Raja Ampat

By Stephen Rickard

Published in 2026 by
Norwood House Press
2544 Clinton Street
Buffalo, NY 14224

Printed in the United States of America

Library of Congress Cataloging-in-Publication Data:
Names: Rickard, Stephen, 1957-, author. | Hawkins, Daisy, author. | Hamilton, Andy, illustrator. | Aloisi, Giuliano, illustrator.
Title: Raja ampat / written by Stephen Rickard. Was that today? / written by Daisy Hawkins, illustrated by Andy Hamilton. Escape / written by Stephen Rickard, illustrated by Giuliano Aloisi.
Description: Buffalo, NY : Norwood House Press, 2026. | Series: Phonics all-stars: phase 5a
Identifiers: ISBN 9781978578869 (pbk.) | ISBN 9781978578876 (library bound) | ISBN 9781978578883 (ebook)
Subjects: LCSH: Reading–Phonetic method–Juvenile fiction. | English language–Phonetics–Juvenile fiction. | Indonesia–Juvenile fiction. | Prehistoric peoples–Juvenile fiction. | Extraterrestrial beings–Juvenile fiction.
Classification: LCC LB1573.3 R534 2026 | DDC 372.465–dc23

CPSIA compliance information: Batch #CW26NHP: For further information contact Norwood House Press at 1-800-237-9932.

Welcome to Raja Ampat.

This part of the planet is such a treat to visit.

People say it is the best spot to see all sorts of sea life.

Come with me to see some of the things that inhabit this part of the planet.

The seas near Raja Ampat are teeming with all sorts of fish.

This is a **manta ray**.

Some people say it is a **devilfish**, as it has little "horns," but the manta ray is not a devil.

In fact, as a rule, it is as meek as it looks.

When you were little, you might have seen a fish like this in a film.

It is a **clownfish**. It looks just as bright as a painted clown.

You can see clownfish at
the bottom of the sea,
hidden in the weeds.

This is a **blue sea star**. You can see that it is clinging to a reef that is not so deep.

Look how clear the sea is!

What do you think this is?

If you'd have asked me, I'd have said it was a discarded pot.

In fact, it's an **ink spot sea squirt**.

One end is fixed to a rock, and it waits for food to come to it. (No, it's not teeth that you can see – they are a sort of filter.)

"What is this?" I hear you say.

It's a **wobbegong**. That's a sort of shark.

For some people, it is a **carpet shark**, as you will meet it sitting on the sea bed, just like a carpet.

This sort of crab can be seen in Raja Ampat.

Its shell is as smooth as butter.

This sort of fish looks like a floating brush.

It is saying, "Do not pick a fight with me."

In Raja Ampat, there are stunning critters on the land too. Just look at this. It is not something to be messed with.

Land critters in Raja Ampat needs to be a subject for a new book!

Was That Today?

Written by
Daisy Hawkins

Illustrated by
Andy Hamilton

Mr. Ug was thinking hard. He had something important to do today.

Yet, no matter how important it might be, Mr. Ug had forgotten what it was.

“Oh dear,” said Mr. Ug. “What shall I do?”

Mr. Ug asked his wife what to do.

"You need to check the 'to-do' list in the upper cave," Mrs. Ug said to him. "It might be on the list."

"Yes, dear. That is a good plan!" said Mr. Ug.

On the trail to the upper cave, a rock fell to the ground, just near Mr. Ug's feet.

The rock was on fire.

"How odd," Mr. Ug mused.

Then he continued on his way.

He wanted to get to the cave, to see what it was that he had forgotten.

Further up the trail, Mr. Ug saw a cute little pair of tingpuffs – a boy and a girl.

"How odd," mused Mr. Ug. Tingpuffs **never** left their nests in the cliffs.

With a shrug, he continued on his way.

Further up the trail, Mr. Ug expected to see a pair of noshlings. They used this part of the trail to hunt and feed.

But the noshlings were not there. There was just the stench of sulphur, lots of dust and smoke, and a pair of bingblats.

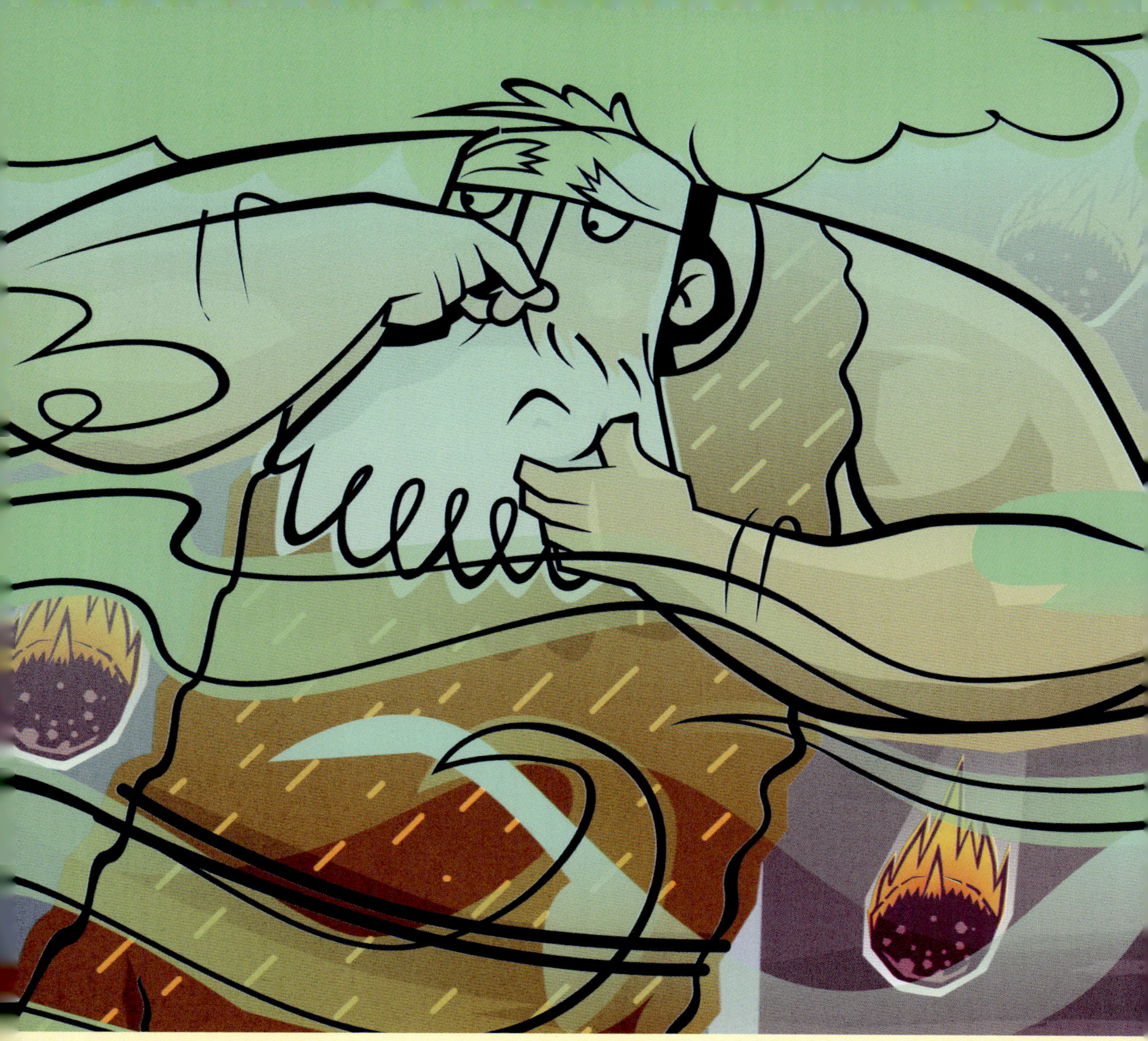

“How odd,” Mr. Ug mused, as he tried not to choke on the fumes.

Then he continued on his way.

In the end, Mr. Ug did reach the upper cave.

He looked at his "to-do" list.

Clean the clubs.

Chop the firewood.

Smoke the meat.

Fix the leak.

"Well, all this stuff has been sorted," he said to himself. "Not one thing has been forgotten."

Feeling smug, Mr. Ug left the cave. He wanted to go home and tell his wife the good news.

At the mouth of the cave, Mr. Ug met an odd sight indeed.

It was a ship. (Mr. Ug did not understand what a ship was, but it looked important.)

The ship was filling up with living things. There was one pair of each of the living things on Mr. Ug's planet.

It looked as if this big ship thing was about to take off.

"Oops," said Mr. Ug. "Was that today?"

Escape

Written by
Stephen Rickard

Illustrated by
Giuliano Aloisi

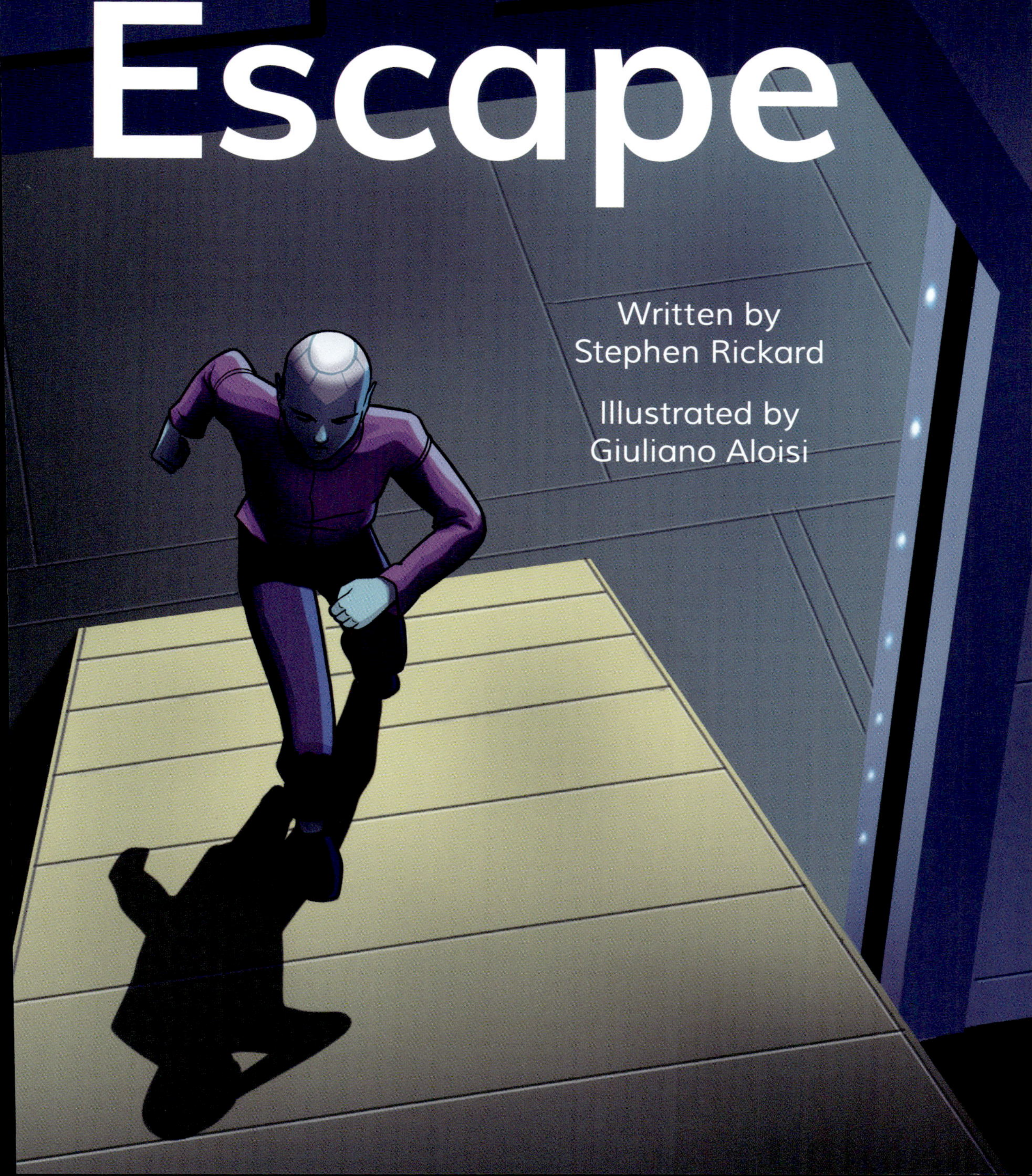

On this planet, there was a tribe of wise beings. They valued life and hope, and did not like to punish people. Crime was not common.

But Varan had breached the rules. He had committed a shocking crime. Now he was under arrest – and he had to submit to the law.
Varan did not expect to go free.
We agree that you did commit this horrific crime. And now you must be punished.
The punishment is life in prison.

Varan is locked up for the night at a starport. In the morning, he will be transported to prison – for life.
This is grim. Now the rest of my life looks so bleak.
I wish I had not committed this crime.

Varan gets some food, then it is lights out.

He must sleep now.

It's not locked! If I'm not spotted, I can escape ...
Hang on! Something is not right. Look – Varan can escape.
Someone made a big mistake!

Varan sneaks out of the prison. He is not spotted.

A starship is parked on the runway.
Can Varan use it to escape?
He leaps into the starship.
This is such good luck!

Inside the starship, Varan has a shock ...

Lift off!

The starship lands on a distant, uninhabited planet.
Landed! I have lots of food and air on this starship. I can stay on this planet as long as I need to.

Varan has escaped. He has avoided a life in prison.

Back on Varan's home planet, at the starport ...
The punishment has been implemented, sir, just as you asked.
The starship has landed on that distant planet, just as we intended.

The prisoner Varan will now spend the rest of his life alone on that planet.

Good. We took the prisoner's freedom, but we did not take from him the biggest thing that there is in life ...
Hope.